AH, MAN!
A Slim Volume of Poetry

By His Excellency
Apollo Polyhistor Starmule

About The Author

Apollo Starmule is a koan whose life is like the coordinated clapping of many hands.

SATYA YUGA BOOKS ™
Asheville Weaverville Nacogdoches Tokyo

To Vicki,
with thanks

AH, MAN! A Slim Volume of Poetry

ISBN 978-0-9763230-2-0

Cover Designed by Chris Master

Preface

I know very little about anything.   I expand and reflect. I do not know.

My ignorance made this book possible. Knowledge had nothing to do with it. Knowledge gets in the way of knowing, while ignorance befriended and transmuted is the ally of knowing.

Chains are broken and the heart flies free when knowledge is forgotten.

I only know that I *am knowingness*.

I knew a priest once who had been a friend to Alan Watts. This priest was an initiate of his own soul. He said Alan Watts told him, "I'm just trying to keep the people entertained while the Holy Spirit does its work." Amen.

Ah, Man!

Books by Apollo Starmule

UNDO THE WINTER: The Odyssey of Sonny-Bob Culpepper (fiction)

*CRUCIFIXION AND RESURRECTION: A Pamphleteer Speaks
(nonfiction)*

With more releases prophesied, so stay tuned!

'Obscuris vera involvens'
'Sic fulget in umbras'

Refuse
is all that there was
between the slow past
and the fast now.

Refuse.

Ah, Man
tubby is too tight
tubby is too tight for me.

Get a little rest
tubby will reform.
Break him out tomorrow night
sad and sober.
Make him wise up and face life.

Lost a poem
on this goddam fucking computer
that would laugh and laugh
if I explained to it
that it is supposed to make my life easier.

TASTE MY ASS

taste my ass
you fuckin' weirdo capitalist
you fucking cream coloured commie in a nightskirt black and blue from fame
and shame of suckin' on the
capitalist egg of exploitation
cause there ain't no difference between you
no, not really.

Hipster commie
cookie-cutter capitalist
all the same.

Just names
just greed of ego and egg on face
covered up by the coldest cream.

Big Sur Funtowne

yeah, I see you over there, baby
I see you with your pale roses and your bags of sweat
I see the candy up your nose and other things.
I see other things.
I see the things you do when you're a tramp
'cause I be watchin' you, baby.
Yes, yes, I be watchin' you.
Better get you a gun.

WALKIN' CATFISH

yes, yes, I be the one you call on
when you need someone to crawl on
I be the bum on the beach
makin' a castle out of sand.
Fly too high and swim too long, honey
time to crawl back up on the sand
time to crawl to your daddy, mama
like a catfish with lipstick on.

Scrotum Dinette

Hanging off the edge of the chair
my balls swing without fear
and know not the pain of the years.
They know neither preachments
nor sacrifice
they know not the glowing hope of youthful things
which have vanished into the loop of consciousness
having been outgrown.
All is fulfilled
treasures laid bare
and bare and bare and bare
nudity was always my thing, but--
now it doesn't seem to matter.

Behold, the triumph of technology.
When was the last time you did anything without being monitored?

SELIGMAN

. . . another "6" in the roadsign, and I would expect to see the devil herself
surveying me like an armadillo dried and abandoned alongside the road. But
there are only two sixes on the roadsign, so I pull into the motel where Cliff
Robertson stayed and they give me his room. It is a nice room and smells good.
It is pleasing to the eye. I begin to comprehend what Cliff Robertson saw in
Seligman, Arizona.

There are two beds in the room.

I go to the Roadkill Cafe and the lady with the strong arms takes my order. I
have always loved strong women, and this one bulges with muscularity. She is
tall, with dark hair and such radiant strength . . . but the weariness of my
emotional, physical and mental bodies makes it too tough for me to convince her
to seduce me. So I admire her quietly, and I eat. The food is flavourful. I will
always remember this day of eating roadkill in the fall of 1998.

When I see the greatness and value of people I am happy.
For then I know that one day we all will be free.
No prison can hold a god.

LADY LOST

Lady lost her soul today
wasn't strong enough to follow her heart
followed the head,
acted according to preconceptions.
Now she's gone
just an empty shell walking around
pretending to be herself
but her Self is gone.

PATRICIA

I know Patricia in gratitude
I bless her in joy
she is my inspiration
and my strength.
Sometimes, anyway.

The rest of the time I have to make do
with whatever heartfelt impulses
are available to me
from the nexus of existence
where I dwell in peace.

The Artist vs. The Corporation

don't let popular culture trivialize you
make you a fad
humanity is no passing fad.

But Pepsi is
and so are its spokespersons.

LION OF LIBERTY

Oh, all my children
you must be free
I grounded it for you
the lion of liberty.
You must ride the lion's back
convincing yourselves to adore him
he already adores you
and waits to share his bounty
his freedom of Self
with every one of you who bathes himself free of illusion and the corruption of
egotism.
Bathe with me,
oh my children
and let it be more than a bath of mud.

BLUE AND GOLD, HURRAH! HURRAH!

My blue family
I do adore you
and weep blue tears of liquid gold for you.
I trust you
to make the right decisions for your day
for the earth has been quickened now
and no longer fears you
and is learning the wisdom to allow you to exercise yours.

Beyond Even Love, Lies This . . .

Expand with me
I do embrace you
now and forevermore.
I adore you
I embrace you with All That We Are.
I crave nothing
for I have no form
I crave no one
for I touch all formless ones
who have followed me
into the VOID of true existence.
The touch of such a life
is dear
but there is no jeopardy attached
to the sweetness.
The sweetness always just IS
and can never be altered or thwarted.
Touch yourself
touch Me
I am Self.

By and large the press sucks
they devote almost all their attention to the appearance of tragedy
without looking for the reality that lies beneath the appearance.
Such shallow people
how can they look in the mirror
and consider themselves professionals?
Well, it's pretty clear:
they *don't* look in the mirror.

COME, LET US SPEAK OF SUCKING

Let us speak of sucking,
and let us denote that which sucks.
Falsehood sucks.
Love is Truth, and it is Freedom,
so propaganda sucks. Turn off the news.
Rules suck bigtime,
and only a brute needs them.
Rules are based in the world of illusion,
which says others must be controlled.
But oneself must be disciplined by one's Self
and *never* controlled by anything.
One's Self cannot be controlled, anyway.
Not by oneself, or by any external manipulation.
One's Self is beyond rules.
Anarchy Rules!

READY TO FLY

smooth . . . yeah, baby smooth. Feels good.
'Bout to go, 'bout to flow into the next phase.
Phasing, man, phasing. Yaaaaah.
Flip!
See me fly, rolling without punches.
Flowing around everywhere.
I'm a stream, baby. I eddy around rocks.
I let the trout come to me to play. See them play.
One of them flew out of the water to catch a bug. It hung there for a moment.

YADA YADA YADA

damn she is fine
if we had sex
would she yada yada the sex
or the meal?

CLAYBURG

. . . was I born upside down
what world is this
how could I have come to be here?
I don't belong here
or anyplace else within spitting distance.
These people are made of clay
uninvigorated
they don't realize the nature of art
is that the artist breathes life into the clay.

And This Is Why I Scream.

CATEGORIZE THIS

Categorize this
does it give you a thrill
like a dose of sunshine
from an empty pill?
Hubris . . .
if you sleep outside one of your little boxes
how can you rate someone who is awake inside it?
Which box is which?
Anyhow, I've got your category right here, baby.

NAACP

Go inside, kids
don't answer the door
maybe the nightriders will believe
we don't live here no more.
Can't let them see we're proud to be
from South Carolina.
Got to hold our heads down
and shuffle our feet
always look downbeat.
Got to say "Yass, Massa",
to the NAACP.

Slavery's fight
is ours today
as descendants of slaves
try to control what we say.
Try to control what we ARE
take our symbols down
but we don't hate them
we're all just human beings.
And now we're equal in slavery.

'Cause that's what it's about
evening the books
revenge for real and imagined wrongs.
The damn yankees imported the slaves
under British flag, and then the American
the damn yankees sold the slaves to us
but the NAACP never calls for burning
British or American flags.

The NAACP calls the stars and bars
a treasonous flag
conveniently forgetting the United States
was born in a glorious burst of treason
and that Lincoln said he'd keep slavery
if it would save the Union.
He only wanted to save the Union.
But we forgive those persons
from the National Association to Assure Compliance Politically

even as we evade their border patrols.[*]
We empathize with each one of them
and embrace them in the brotherhood of our comman humanity
for we've had a glimpse at what their ancestors went through.
Slavery is an unjustifiable evil in all its forms.

They call our ancestors terrorists at their rallies
then they go out and try to sow terror among us.
Our ancestors weren't terrorists and didn't own slaves
and most of their neighbors didn't own slaves
and when they fought,
they fought for their country.
They weren't fighting for slavery.
Some of the people who did own slaves
were too cowardly to fight for their country
and paid others to fight for them.
Draft dodgers, circa 1860.

We forgive the NAACP
for its violent hatred toward us
and for its attempts to violate
one of our sacred symbols.
Ignorance and hate take many forms.
They don't understand us
and won't see that we mean them no harm.
Yes, the Klan may fly our flag
but the Klan also waves the Christain Cross
and the flag of the United States,
so we're back to the hypocrisy of the NAACP
which masks its hate
through the sanctified pulpit.
After they've destroyed our flag
maybe then they'll turn on their friends
and go after the cross.

---

[*] If you don't live in or near South Carolina, that line may sound insane to you. If that is the case, you're not a member of the NAACP, which at this writing (March, 2002) actually is running border patrols around South Carolina to try to terrorize tourists into going somewhere else to spend their money. The new face of hatred in America.

YOU ARE DIRE

you are dire
with your capitals locked
never changing
your boldfaced, jackbooted approach.
Rigid. Vengeful. Hateful. A sower of separation and glamour.
Well, try sowing this:
I throw cold water on the fires of your illusions.

ET WRITES HOME

It's a poet's paradise here, mom, dad
the people are always drunk on flaming emotion
or sober on cold-heartedness.
There is no balance here
no purity
there's all the things
we poets crave and want to write about.

The truthtellers are disguised as madmen
the madmen pretend to be truthtellers.
The real truthtellers can be found almost anywhere,
except for the talking heads on picture boxes.
The picture boxes are reserved for the mad only.

They hurt
these people hurt.
This is the planet of suffering
to learn compassion.
Logic would dictate accepting this fact
and opening the heart in forgiveness
to both oneself and others.
But few are logical here.
Most simply rationalize and pretend it is logic.

There is a fire here
and a gunblast
searing across everything I am
or might ever be
and I am wounded and burned.
Their trauma units cannot deal with the hurt I feel.
If they could, maybe they wouldn't need me.

HERD MENTALITY

. . . yasss, we go down to the soda shop
the soda shop, the soda shop
we go down to the soda shop
that's where everyone plays.

Now we go salute the flag
salute the flag, salute the flag
now we go salute the flag
that's where everyone plays.

Now let's go burn the books
burn the books, burn the books
now let's go burn the books
that's where everyone plays.

Now let's go jail the fags
jail the fags, jail the fags
now let's go jail the fags
that's where everyone plays.

Now let's go destroy the guns
destroy the guns, destroy the guns
now let's go destroy the guns
so nobody can fight the herd.

AMOEBA

Yes, we were amoebas.
In those days, we had nothing that could be called self-awareness.
Just a universe without borders, with no "I" in the middle.
No "I" anywhere.
We were content.

Then we became dogs.
We learned from our masters to be more conscious.
"We" became "I", to a certain degree.
We were still content, because we had our Gods.
We were reasonably at peace.

Then we became humans.
Suffering was all we knew.
We evolved into Hell.
No more Gods except those made in the image of our own egotism.
We writhed in agony.

Then we took the next step . . .
we still look human, but we're not.
We evolved into Bliss.
We have our God
and our God is LOVE.

DARK AMERICAN CHAMBER

Their lack of compassion is their only judge
for prosecuting that sick woman
who, under the influence of unfathomable illness
destroyed her family.

But no family is truly destroyed
each family lives together in eternity
no matter what seeming disaster is brought to them
in the world of form.

This woman and her family
gave the alleged authorities a chance
to begin to learn the supreme virtue of compassion.
The authorities are very fortunate the universe is compassionate
and will devise an appropriate programme
for them to begin to master this difficult subject.

suffering is not the purpose of life
compassion is.
the hammer is not the purpose of construction
the house is.

BENNIE HAS THE SHITS

. . . I bitch at Bennie because he left the toiletries in disarray
I'm afraid to touch my toothbrush.
We need some aromatherapy here.
Don't poot no more, Bennie. I've had enough.

It is not glamourous when Bennie walks into the room
after his bowel movement
followed by a slim brown odour.
That odour sends me out the door
and down the street
to breathe the odour of a fresh old tree.

MILK TO MEAT VIA ALCHEMY

Hi ya, sweet Francis man
why did your mom name you Francis?
Was old Queenie trying to raise a girley girl?
Maybe she knew you'd have a fondness for flower arranging,
and a talent for avoiding the thorns . . .
though bearded, you certainly possess feminine wiles.
Hey, people think nothing of it
you are a sociable fellow
and quite upper class
riding in a two door carriage.
I'll bet there's no confusion around the names you use.
Heh, heh.
Wasn't Francis the name of Ronald Reagan's mule?
Or was it the other way around?
Scratch your beard over that one
you mulish rogue
never giving up
never giving an inch
despite overwhelming odds.
Learning to step around
in order to step on and crush.
I like that. Chicken soup for the Anarchist's soul.
Belch.
God Bless America.

FREEDOM MAN

BOAT OF CONSCIOUSNESS
I arrive late, but not too late. Now for the next
few thousand years I'll be busy.
Like a shell upon the shore I come,
filled with Holy Will, and radiating Divine Love.
Lying there, waiting for my turn.
Waiting for the current of the Loveforce
to pick me up and deposit me where needed.
The stream of Earthly existence.
I don't have long to wait.

I shudder, and am filled with new life.
I sigh, then begin to roar and roar and roar . . .
I had been led to believe my assignment would be lovely.
Maybe I'd misled myself by staring at the pictures
of the great blue sphere of Earth.
I just had to look at those damn pictures . . .
Well, now it's too late. Got to make the best of it.

There is ugliness all around. Beauty, too,
but I've been assigned to work with the inmates of this place,
and they suck. They devote most of their attention
to creating more ugliness. And I have to clean up after them.
Jesus H. Christ. I'm a janitor.
Got to convince these people to clean up after their own damned selves.

FREEDOM
The most astounding thing about this Earth is that the inmates
don't know what Freedom is.
They've never encountered it,
never even heard of it.
Never seen the palest reflection of it.
They are fair game for the status quo.
"Damn," I mumble, wiping my brow,
"It'll take thousands of years just to make a dent
in this fucking status quo."
For the umpteenth time
I curse my choice of assignment,
but then I remember:
I chose this work in Perfect Freedom
and Perfect Love.
I have nothing to bitch about.
Taking responsibility for our own choices

is an early step towards Freedom.
How could I have forgotten that?

ROSES
A few hearts bloom in private
down thru the long ages.
Just a few.
Just enough
to keep the Earth wobbling along
and never quite falling into the chaos of unquickened matter.
Unquickened matter does provide the majority of the experiences here
but the Band of Brothers somehow begins to thrive
in spite of the surroundings.
Sometimes a seed can grow out of a rock,
then gradually bust the rock.
We'll see.

PERSONALITIES
The work thru the long ages
causes both an increase of soul force
and an internal diversification of personality.
Ooooops! Big challenge, here. Got to cope
with a blossoming of personality. Never
expected this. Back home there's not so
many internal selves; we're a different breed.
On this Earth, though, I'm developing many personalities.
Gonna be a bitch to try to unify all these babies.
Hard to tell if the personalities help or hinder the WORK.
Flow together, damn it!
Unify!
Get it done.

COYOTES
The Band of Brothers turns to the Coyote for inspiration,
and to the Fox.
Have to, to survive.
Personality diversification continues,
and it helps in our survival.
Back home we don't need such subterfuge,
but here it becomes essential.
Unification . . . not yet.
But eventually.

AMERICA
In recorded history, there is none like Her. She becomes our home,

and She is the inspiration of the whole Earth.
Everyone who can come to her
does come to her
to be embraced by her love and by
the first faint spark of Freedom.
The little flame is in the open now.
It is the beginning of our time
and we can be a little bolder.

FEELIN' BLUE
In a blue cloak they come
the children of our efforts
down the long centuries.
They flow into the Earth,
and especially into America
and theirs is the destiny of the ages.
We have primed them in their many ventures here
and we welcome also some who come from far away
and who may have never set foot here until now.
We welcome them all, and our hearts rejoice at last.
The end is not in sight, but the beginning surely is.

DOUBLE-OUGHT SEVEN

Curmudgeon
lofty and bearded
where is your wizard's cap?
Shhhhhh! Quiet, child. Don't let them hear.
Last thing I need is a mob chasing my mortal frame around the lake.
Mustn't get distracted
work to do.
Here's a volume you may enjoy
it'll help you learn the subtleties
of masking art with art
to save your bacon.
If I serve as the link, child,
between bacon and bacon
does that make me sausage?

Golden-Skinned Girl

Golden-skinned girl
I recognize an aspect of myself in you
and I see why
women were sometimes worshipped in ancient cultures.
I want to worship you today
you bring out that old, natural instinct
you are refined, pure
a beacon of both flesh and light
and I admire your courage.

To perform as you do
in the flesh and little else
requires extremes of courage
unknown by most women,
whose unfortunate dependance on the status quo
keeps them unacquainted with most forms of prostitution.

But you have the advantage
nothing can hold you back
nothing ever has or will.
As you shine and shine before the world
I only hope you will not forget where you came from.
The energy shining from you
is testament to your Divine Birth
combining soul and flesh with growing precision.
Remember always your Self
and let your breasts continue swaying to the beat of your heart
rather than the glamour of the fervid moment.

I LIVED IN TEXAS

I lived in Texas,
a great big state
full of great big karma for me.
Most of that will go unreported.
I would like to mention, however,
that I met a friend there from a previous life
and I think the credit is hers more than mine
that we did not repeat the mistakes of the past.

THERE IS NO MONOPOLY ON HEALING

They debased the prostitutes of old
and destroyed their temples
suddenly nature became sinful
and WOMAN made to shirk Her natural function
of serving as healer and soother of trauma.
Police states arose
the strong arm of the sword
lost the connection to nature
that provides a warrior's wisdom
and the ability to regain peace.
The rage and pain of unbalanced religion
substituted for the warm touch of the Goddess
and this wrathful fire destroyed our common humanity.
The earth was destroyed by fire,
Jehovah's fire of repression
Allah's fire of subservience.
Jesus was ignored. They remembered only His name,
but not the man Himself.

This trap was probably devised
by insane men who worshipped only war,
or their insecure wives, who wanted a monopoly on prostitution,
fearing they couldn't compete with the professional healers.
One John to one Whore. The principle of sharing was lost.
Greed and grasping carried over into every arena of life.
The very foundation of the bodily temple became an
object to be grasped and hoarded, instead of embraced with love,
so the natural sharing of the warm chalice of passion
was replaced by the cold hatred of rape and seduction
and force and duplicity carried over into every aspect of life.
Frenetic commerce was born. As some grasp for luxury and accumulate
far more than they can ever use, children starve.
They starve because the warm touch of the Goddess was lost,
She who soothed our wounded spirits and taught us to share.

WARRIOR, COME HOME

Warrior, come home
tears for you were shed
and shed and shed and shed.
When you return
tears alone will not be enough
to wash you clean.
That will take time.
The duty of the healer
complements your duty to justice.
The duty of the healer
is a duty to you.
Let the healer do her duty
as the brittle strength that served you so well
slips away in the flood of the strength of your Greater Self
that pours thru you with the healer's encouragement.
Brittle strength will no longer serve.
You need no more endure the unendurable
as you find your Self.
Your Self is far bigger than any foe you have ever faced
or ever will face.
Your Self is your natural home.
Warrior, come home.

I STAND NAKED IN THE GARDEN
AND SING A SONG TO YOU

Breasts, full and ripe
the sweetest fruit to grace my sight
my lips sigh in an agony of bliss.
You came to me when I was naked
as I presently am
having just dropped my robe
before your inviting gaze.
Your jerkin, undone with gentle fingers
hangs loosely
and the fabric of your blouse falls away
to reveal that which I worship
in the one whom I adore.
For I adore you.

There were times
so long ago when I forgot you
other times, more recent
when I tried to control you.
I control you no more,
and accept the forgiveness you extend to me.
I was wrong.

You cannot be controlled
nor should it ever be attempted.
Why should a smile be controlled?
or the opening of the sweetest wildflowers.
Nothing should ever be controlled,
and you are Everything. You are All.
You are Free,
and in trying to control you
I only controlled me.

THE SONGS THE ANGELS WANT TO SING

These are the songs the angels want to sing
I hear the flowing rustle of their wings
hovering about me,
coaching me,
urging me without respite
to put new paint on old houses.

They hold a cup of gold to my bloodstained lips
and ask that I drink,
that the blood may become wine.
Their virtue seeks expression,
but its fullest expression must ever come
thru one who has suffered the evils of crucifixion,
then risen to tell about it.

These days will draw to a close
and in a far distant time
when angels mingle freely with the earthborn
there will be no more need for crucifixion.
When the marriage of Heaven and Earth is complete
all beings will hear the song of the angels,
and each being will be a part of that song.

SONG OF FORGIVENESS

I hear a bell
around the neck of a lamb
I hear the roaring of a lion.
Both approach me in the thicket.

I burned this section of ground
a long time ago.
I cleared it,
thinking to raise a crop.
But only thorns grew here after I burned it.

I haven't really been nourished for a long time.

There have been times lately
when I have wept
seeing my daughters and wives turned into plastic.
After the thorns grew
they changed, grew cool.
Their touch became prickley
and drew blood.
I shudder at the sight of the blood they draw out of me.
I try to avoid them now, but I cannot.
They know my haunts,
they always know where to find me.

I dine on thorns
and my women pull the blood from my veins.
I spit blood onto the ground
and it spits and hisses like fire.

When the thorns came my women changed.
They blamed me for the thorns
and for the lack of nourishment.
They became plastic, and they grew thin.
They were no longer women, not really.
Everyone's women changed. And none of us
have women anymore.

The lion comes, roaring along like he has a mouthful of wool.
He seems hesitant, undecided, as he steps into the clearing
where I huddle, clutching my knees on the ground.
He sits down on his haunches and surveys me.
I expect to see him spit out some wool,

but to my surprise, the lamb steps into the clearing.
"I tore off my bell," he sniffs, by way of explanation.
"It didn't suit me anymore."
Then the lamb glances at the lion.

When the lamb sits down
I begin to cry.
Both lion and lamb scoot closer to me.
"What's the matter, Bub?" growls the lamb.
"Speak up! Don't tell me the cat got yer tongue."

"The women . . . " I wail.

"There are no more women," the lion says. "I wish I could say I ate them all,
but I didn't. They just vanished."

"Yes . . . " I say, "they became plastic and brittle. They aren't real anymore."

The lamb gestures with his head to his right,
which is my left: "That one's real," he says, his eyes growing a tad wide.

My breath catches as She steps into the thicket.
Regal, a lady in a crown of sparkling leaves,
her Pagan nudity filling up the whole sky,
untamed, but obviously not undisciplined.
Wild, but beautifully refined and sweet.
Powerful. Powerful.

Where the sword comes from I do not know
but suddenly it is in her hand,
point extended towards me
as though for an annointing.
Or a beheading.

Suddenly her cheeks turn to rose
and she laughs,
a cheery, sparkling, lovely sound,
and all my senses are elevated into a new dimension.
I smile candidly.

When have I ever smiled candidly?

When she opens her mouth to speak
something like a breath of dogwood petals
freshens the stale air of the thicket.

The gloom begins to lift.
"I don't think there'll be a beheading today, my love,"
she whispers. "Or any day. For I have
always loved you. Even when you have forgotten me,
I have always loved you. I always will love you,
my friend."

She reverses the sword and comes to me,
then extends the haft. "It is yours," she breathes.
I accept the great sword as her breath freshens me.
I haven't been nourished in so long,
my whole body shakes violently and my cells
scream in an agony of sweet relief.
The sweetest relief.
She is with me again.

The lion and lamb glance at one another and wink,
then disappear.

WOMEN LIKE POETS

I am a buoy at sea
and the women swirl around me
foaming, foaming.

I glisten from the foam.
We glisten together.

Women like poets.

ORANGE

I am an orange person today
I have been black
and white
and all the rest of it.
Today I am orange.

Where is my refuge?
The NAACP will not defend me
for I am not black.
Whitey doesn't understand me
and doesn't want to.
The other flavors
have an attitude similiar to Whitey
and his black friends.
But when there are enough of us,
we will have our own organization
and our own logo.
Our violent friends in the streets
our apparently civilized friends in Congress.
We will go to war against the other flavors.
That future war could be prevented
if only I had refuge among the other flavors
TODAY.

ROOT

She knelt before me praying
as I ate my crackers.
"Root," she breathed,
tears in her eyes,
"thou art my turgid god."

"That's nice, honey,"
I said, noting that her attentions
had aroused my member
as her tongue played flag
to my pole.

I have never fully understood
her religious aspirations.

NUNNERY OF THE ROOT

Lost in a golden forest
I came upon the Nunnery of the Root.
They allow Root Worship here,
they positively promote it.
A leftover vortex of energy from Pagan times,
perhaps, encouraged the nuns to sport about the Phallus.

It wasn't yet Mayday,
but it didn't have to be.
The nuns selected a new Maypole every day
and the uses they put it to
were much more versatile
than any uses of a traditional Maypole.
A real Maypole is just too huge!

The nuns didn't stop there, though.
Not enough men came thru this golden forest
to supply all the poles needed for all the nuns
on a daily basis,
so the nuns frequently made do with one another,
according to the custom of the regular convents.
But they were much more open about their gaiety
than the lacivious and lewd nuns of the Christain faith.
The Christain nuns were always too repressed
to enjoy their sport with total gusto.
But this was not the case
at the Nunnery of the Root.

The Mother Superior languidly greeted me,
and stroked my thigh as two of her daughters
acquainted themselves with the presence of
that which they worshipped. They saw
that I was indeed a carrier
of the Holy Relic,
and they smacked over it,
each one offering a tongue bath
to my saintly instrument.
They made me spurt myself
upon the Holy Mother
and she accepted with humility
and joy
the annointing of my sanctified lovehead.

Her daughters had no habits, I saw,
save the habit of offering the burning bush freely.
I frequently accepted. And I was there forty days and forty nights.

When I left the Nunnery of the Root
I knew that a new crop of descendants
would grow up after me. For I
had impregnated some of the ladies.
For I had come to see them as ladies,
rather than as nuns.
They were far more generous than regular nuns,
and more in tune with nature.
They knew that crucifixion, while sometimes necessary,
should never be celebrated for its own sake.
So they didn't worship the cross.
They worshipped God.

And they came to know their God
the God of Love,
through their constantly dripping passion,
their dripping, dripping chalices
pouring forth from out of the depths of themselves
their dedication and devotion.
They were real ladies,
not like the dried up pretend ladies
who play at knowing God
then reject some of His manifestations.

They did not martyr themselves without reason.
Martyrdom was not a way of life for them.
They might get killed in the line of duty
if discovered by the primary society
but they certainly didn't seek it out.
The nuns and priests and other sanctimonious nuts
of the primary society were pretend martyrs
lost in a sort of codependant hypocrisy
where they tortured themselves without reason,
glorying in a crucifix they didn't understand,
then in the dark places, touching themselves for a few moments'
forbidden pleasure. Even the nipple of a Christain nun
must occasionaly yield to the desire for stimulation
and don't get me started about the clitorious.
And everyone has heard about the abuse
the priests and nuns of Christainity engage in.

But the ladies at the Nunnery of the Root
had foresworn the infringing lifestyles
and methods of the mainstream.
The Root ladies were pure.
Reasonably pure, anyway. The
occasional case of gonorreah was easily dealt with.

And so my Holy Relic and I continue our travels
and I keep an eye out for another golden forest.
In the golden forest,
my golden bough is all the currency I need.

TRIBUTE TO APHRODITE

I know that sometimes I am crude
though She is refined.
My vulgarity was born out of Christainity,
a religion as far from its Founder
as the far galaxies are from earth.
You do not give a gun to an infant to play with,
yet the infants of the Christain "faith" play with
an instrument far more dangerous than any gun could ever be,
even a gun in the hands of a psychotic infant who has a speed loader.

The instrument of the cross is the weapon the Christains use
to torture themselves and others in their quest for unholy hypocrisy.
They have hurt many and helped damned few.
Even when they are allegedly trying to help someone,
that damned cross of theirs is somewhere in the background
giving off the aroma of rotting flesh those people are so fond of.
They lack the perception to see
that the crucifixion on Golgotha
was only the outermost symbol of Jesus' real crucifixion,
which is far more excruciating than any form of physical torture.
The crucifixion on Golgotha
was a piece of cake for Jesus.
He would laugh and laugh
if he visited a Christain church today
and saw the use those people have made of the cross.
He would be doubled over in hysterics
gasping for breath
if he saw their long faces as they solemnly recite
the trials of the supposed crucifixion.
The crucifixion on Golgotha
was only the smallest part of the crucifixion.
Less than the tip of an iceberg.
Just a symbol, because Jesus lived a life of symbols.
Symbols are how we communicate.
Yes, he was crucified on Golgotha,
but those who crucified him never saw the real crucifixion.
That vision and experience are only granted to those few
who do the Work. The nature of the Work
is kept secret from the insincere. They will never know.

OUTBREAK OF PERVERSION

Just saw on the news
how they'd apprehended two more Catholic priests
who screw boys.
Boys too young to drink,
too young to own a weapon,
too young to drive.
Boys too young even
to be interested in girls.

This is the nature of perversion:
It starts when the religious impulse
tries to stamp out the life of sex.
The life of sex cannot,
WILL NOT
be stamped out.
Could you stamp out your sexuality?
Then what makes you think your priest
can stamp out his?
He can't. All he can do is lie about it.
Hypocrisy is all that's left to him . . .
hypocrisy and abuse.

You can't get spiritual results
from an unnatural religion
and the Catholic religion is unnatural.
The spiritual life
is fueled by the sexual life.
Where there is no sexual life
the spiritual life is frustrated also,
and both become warped and confused.
The individual becomes twisted and perverted,
and if he's not already a Catholic priest
he will certainly want to become one.

So Catholic priests furtively return
to their sexuality
but when they get there
it's too late.
No positive reclamation is possible
as long as they continue to wear the collar.
So in their need and their frustration
they hurt others. They hurt the weakest and littlest

ones they can find, and intimidate them into silence.
The Catholic Church has always been set up
to intimidate and to silence. And it will
be run this way as long as it exists.
It cannot be salvaged.

If you have children
and you are raising them in the Catholic Church
surely you must have some idea by now
of the terrible chance you are taking.
Is the Catholic Church worth the lives of your kids?
Any person who remains a Catholic
in light of present knowledge
cannot pretend to be blameless
when they find another innocent has been abused.
To support Catholicism
is to support abuse,
just as law-abiding, taxpaying Germans
supported the concentration camps.
To hide one's head in the sand
is to sanction abuse and degradation of children.
The problem won't be solved by
getting rid of a few so-called celibate priests
who have been caught performing acts of sexual abuse.
You will have to get rid of all the priests.
You will have to vacate this unnatural religion and let it collapse.
You can find a better religion.
Children deserve a better religion,
and they deserve elders who are
natural men and women
who live guileless lives.

WORLD SAVIOR

Do not be wicked
Mary's little lamb,
do not be naughty
and do not fail.
Do not be deceived
by the goat of cloven hoof
whose primary desire
is to see you fail.
To see lamb become goat
is a primary jest for that one.
Embarrass him
reject the cloven hoof
even if it means
facing your own darkness
to drive him into the light.

HIGH SOCIETY

Every society is high on something,
usually fear.
The fear will create many symptoms,
many devices so it can spread itself.
Laws are fear-based.

Everyone fears death
because the Catholic Church edited reincarnation out of the Bible
and made it appear that you only get once chance
and if you flub that chance
you'll go to hell forever.

But you've already been in hell forever
because of your fear.
Fear has not been the companion,
it has been the ruler of the species
for as long as humanity has existed on earth.

Fear is an illusion.
It is based in the illusion of mortality.
But there is no mortality,
just a changing of clothes
from time to time.

DO YOU DARE TOUCH YOURSELF?

Are you afraid to be frank
on account of what some priest might think
or because of what some puffed up egotist in a suit
might say . . . an egotist who makes his living from a controlling system,
by the way, and who can be counted on to preserve the system at all costs?
Are you afraid of these people and what they think? Why?

You would not be afraid of such people
if you took the time to get to know yourself.
These people know only the smallest aspect of themselves,
so if you took the time to get to know some of your bigger aspects
you would find that you dwarf the priests and media people
and government workers.
You dwarf them all.
Ultimately, you might even begin to feel compassion for them
because they've chosen to lock themselves
into such a tiny, tiny prison.

At that point
you would be free.

FISH

Little fish in a great big pool
you know you have it coming
the pool is being drained
and you have no place to go.

Well, there is one place that would accept you,
but you have to hurry.
There is a jar,
a great pitcher,
that brims with holy water.
Fresh holy water.

GIVE A KID A CIGARETTE

Give a kid a cigarette,
give a kid a gun
turn him loose in a car
let him have his fun.
Don't require a helmet
when he rides his bike
but hand him a condom
when he goes out tonight.

Let the kid know liberty
let him learn to choose
if you hand him restriction
he will only learn to lose.
Set a good example
you don't have to smoke
though if you're living natural
you may be a lusty bloke.

Society is illusion
it is all based on fear
let the kid see confidence
and know that love is near.
Then he'll make his choices
and some may be bad
but he'll love you for the freedom
that he's always had.

Freedom fights control
as control stifles love
to thrive today you need
to be both hawk and dove.
Destroy the illusions
that separate and cause fear
raise a generation
that accepts that love is near.

Give a kid a cigarette
hand a kid a gun
make sure he has his condoms

when he goes out for fun.
Trust in your own heart
to raise children without fear
it's in your best interests
for you're raising your own peers.

PHYSICIAN, HEAL THYSELF

"That's one more thing you'll have to lie to your doctor about,"
sighs a weary mom in her child-rearing column.
Yes . . . "That's one more thing you'll have to lie to your doctor about."
I couldn't have put it any better.

Who are these doctors, anyway, that we should be subject to their judgements?
Are they brilliant creative geniuses? Are they the ones who made the earth
begin to spin?
No.

They are simple little people,
most of them,
whose memories were good enough to get them thru medical school,
so they could begin to "win thru intimidation."
They don't know how to win by being authentic.
Memory . . . that's all most have going for them.
Most creative people wouldn't be able to get thru medical school, but if you
have a good enough memory, you too can graduate
from medical school and sit in judgment on your fellow
human beings.

Watch out! Some of your fellow human beings are creative,
and you won't know what to make of that
so you'll fall back on your platitudes and judgments
like a textbook that has been written a thousand times.

Clunky old emotions
dragging me sometimes,
sometimes I drag them.
Like a Franklin stove,
heavy,
they tire me out.
Discipline,
purification--
NOT repression--
will lead me to the expansion of energy
and I will be absorbed into newness.
My Franklin stove
will become a shiny new space heater.

1950

Hey, cat--you feelin' beat, man?

Naw. I ain't feelin' beat. Just
a little ragged, is all.

I heard that, kitty cat. I be
one hell of a doggy dog, man,
but I ain't got enough spice no
more. You diggin' me? I
ain't got no spice. Gimmie
some spice and I'll be
right there with ya.

Doggie dog, ain't you got no sense?
Nobody got no spice no more, man.
Ain't nobody got it.
Done exhausted the spice. Now
we got to start usin' the fuel, man. You
know, the real stuff.

Kitty cat, I ain't got no real stuff--

Shut yo mouth, doggy dog.
Everbody's got the stuff, man,
but don't nobody know it.
Listen:
what's the sound of
one hand clapping?

Don't know, furry kitten. I never heard
such trash.

Look in the mirror, doggie dog. Chase your tail.

INDIGO CHILDREN

Yeah, it's a blue baby
made in the image of Buddha.
What we goin' to do with it?

Can't have no Buddhas runnin' around, man.
Interfere with business. Make it hard
to sell hamburgers and jewelry, y'know?

I know. Them Buddhas ain't worth a damn.
Meddle in ever'body's business
like there ain't no tomorrow.
We got to think of the future.
Got to serve the future, man. Let's
smother this little Buddha
before he has a chance to ruin the future.
Gimmie that pillow . . .

There. It's done. One for us, zero for Buddha.
Heh, heh, heh . . . Uh-oh!
Did I just hear another baby cry?

A BREEZY RIDE THROUGH DUNSMUIR
ON A CAPITALIST TRAIN

Ain't got no words, Pierre.
Ain't got no words for that dirty trout river.
At a funeral, somebody ought to say some words.

I know, Jean-Paul. I
ain't got no words, neither.
All's I got is a thirst
and no clean water to drink.
That damn train . . .
if they'd a made the railroad company
reinforce that trestle when it was built . . .

Yeah . . . this never woulda happened.
But the railroad didn't want to spend
the money, and now every trout
between Dunsmuir and Shasta Lake
is dead. If them railroad people
had to make a livin' off this river
like them people in Dunsmuir, they
never woulda been no trainload
of chemicals spilled in this river. I'd like
to make them railroad people swallow
a mouthful of chemicals, and
watch them die like a trout.

Be careful, Jean-Paul! Don't
want to hurt nobody's feelin's, do we?

Well, I reckon not, Pierre. Say, remember that
river otter we used to watch in the evenings?
Well, he's laying over there dead.

KRAMER

. . . secret Zen master disguised as doofus . . .
Jerry, Elaine and George,
his secret disciples
meeting for zazen in Jerry's apartment.

Hello, Newman. Devient smirk
of rogue priest. Fat little imp.
Kramer will stop you
in his own good time.

Kramer rolls with Chaos,
then arises out of the Void
to redeem his precincts.

His disciples, asleep in the garden,
never realize they are dreaming.
So Kramer uses his imagination
to set the stage for all their lives.

KRAMER, THE AWAKENED ONE!

Nothing is all there is.

THE DAWNING OF THE VISION

Rooty toot toot
a Druid on a horn
rooty toot toot
a new day is born.

ID:

"Adjust fire, shift onto Apollo
it's his turn now . . .
Kill for peace!
Yee Haaaaaaaa!
Kill for peace!"

APOLLO:

"Cease fire, ID! Cease fire, I say!
What the hell have I
ever done to you?"

Rooty toot toot
a Druid on a horn
rooty toot toot
a new day is born.

ID:

"What haven't you done to me,
you whey-faced bastard?
The next time you try to step on someone,
remember this: 'Repression
Creates Perversion'.
Continue firing, my boys in Lincoln green!
Keep firing!"

In the folds of her vagina,
secretly hidden from the madmen
lay a haunch of venison.
The madmen of Apollo--
for all gods go mad and lose their lustre
after a season of waxing--
played the fiddle as she smiled.
They thought she wanted it,
the knew she would take it.
She always had before.
They held out the rod of cold and perfect steel . . .

somewhere in the distance the Druid played his horn.
They could not hear it, not yet. But
they would. The Lady cocked a sensitive ear,
as she massaged the vagina where the haunch of venison lay.

Rooty toot toot
a Druid on a horn
rooty toot toot
a new day is born.

The earth walks on fire and is burned.
The scabs of pain ooze pus. Volcanoes
erupt. The lady catches her breath. The Druid plays on.

The madmen of Apollo kiss the sacred chalice
wherin lies the haunch of venison.
They kiss the chalice that they hate.
They have to kiss it,
they cannot stop themselves.
But they wish they didn't need it.
So they conquered it long ago . . .
or did they?

Rooty toot toot . . .

"What was that!" cries the bard of Apollo,
whose cold music soothes
only the dead. He
is the first to feel the fear
as he senses his demise. For
dead music cannot conquer live.

Rooty toot toot . . .

He screams and throws his energy
into learning new notes, but
it is too late. His decaying instrument
falls apart on the bed.
For the first time,
the woman laughs.

Pooty poot poot . . . sobs the bard of Apollo . . .
pooty poot poot . . .
he breathes his last in a sigh of regret.
He could have spent the last

two thousand years learning to love.
Now he can only expel foul gases.
He is a dead rose,
and he sobs as he dies.
He is dead.

Rooty toot toot
a Druid on a horn
rooty toot toot
a new day is born.

"Where is the owl
whose wise grace redeems us
and who prompts us
to shake the spear of defiance
at those who would oppress us?"
cries the Lady. Then the owl comes,
and for the first time in a million years
she gazes back into those knowing eyes,
back and back and back . . . back to
when she and the owl were young,
all those millions of years ago. It is her time again,
and it is the time of the owl.

Rooty toot toot . . .

The owl flies to her shoulder
and they both smile. Then they break out
into great peals of laughter, laughter so deep
it hurts their insides. The guardians of Apollo
are aghast. Some flee the room. But one . . . no, it is not
a guardian, it is Apollo himself . . . picks up the steel wand
he has gouged her with before. He licks his lips.
He knows she wants it . . . she always has before . . . nothing
like a pestle for the mortar, heh heh.
"But really," he says upon reflection, "I don't care
if you want it or not. You're going
to get it, anyway."

For the first time
an insane glint comes into Apollo's eye.
The Lady and the owl stop laughing.
They watch him carefully. His
insanity has always been so carefully controlled
it has hardly seemed

like insanity at all. Really,
this particular god always seemed to
have it together, in his ruthless implacable fashion.
No insane glints, and no sane joys.
He'd always been the perfect god,
until he felt the Druid approach.

Suddenly, Apollo screams! He
launches himself at the Lady
whose fingers fly back to her vagina
and pull back the hidden folds.
The haunch of venison,
never suspected by Apollo,
begins to writhe with life. Into a great
stag it changes, and it leaps out
of her vagina onto the charging
god with the perfect rod of steel. It
leaps onto Apollo and gouges him
with its long-tined antlers
as the Druid plays outside their window:

Rooty toot toot . . .

Mad, screaming with pain and fear
at the assault of this uncontrollable beast,
Apollo throws down his steel wand
and cowers in foetal position on
the floor, trying vainly to cover himself
as the beast gouges him with wierd antlers.
A great tine is stuck in Apollo's chest; it
breaks off from the rack of the stag,
whose bloodthirst is satisfied at last.
The stag sits on his haunches beside
the bed, breathing heavily,
waiting to see what Apollo will do.

Rooty toot toot
a Druid on a horn
rooty toot toot
a new day is born.

Apollo lies dying. For
the first time in a long time,
the Lady begins to feel compassion for
him.

She has never really understood him,
but she starts to realize
that if she had understood him
it would have been far easier to fight his tyranny.
Her breath catches in her perfumed throat,
the throat that was about to sing as the beast gouged Apollo--
but now she doesn't feel like singing. A sadness
rises in her throat, and a tear comes to her eye.

Rooty toot toot . . .

She feels like throwing a shoe out
the window at the Druid. **HER** Druid.
She pauses and collects herself; she
could never in good conscience strike
one of her own.
So the Druid plays on.

Rooty toot toot
a Druid on a horn
rooty toot toot
a new day is born.

Surprising herself,
she descends the bed and approaches the fallen god.
Any thirst for vengeance has subsided. She
grows, now: she sees plainly
that vengeance will keep them locked in a cycle
of hate and control and desperation,
and that victory for either is impossible
in such a cycle. "For two specimens of Divinity,
we certainly are slow to catch on," she
murmers as she strokes his hair.

"Yes . . ." he gasps, as his chest
makes sucking sounds, "but I don't
want to understand you. I
am afraid. You scare the hell
out of me."

"Likewise, Apollo. But I just realized I don't want to
win against you anymore. If I win this war,
you'll win the next one. There has to
be a better way."

"Right . . ." he gurgles, in the throes of Death,
knowing that Death is not permanent
and that he'll be back.
"Remind me of this conversation
when I return."

"I will, my love," she whispers. She kisses his forehead, and he dies in her
arms.

Rooty toot toot
a Druid on a horn
rooty toot toot
a new day is born.

FAIRYLAND

There is a place
of profound gaiety
full of pretty ladies
brimming with zeal
who are immune to jealousy.

There is a place
where I am at peace . . .
massaging my heart is a pretty girl
bubbling over with laughter
as I bathe in her joy.

FUNDAMENTALISM

Fundamentalism is an insidious pattern
that crops up in the most unexpected places.
For a while I attended a "New Age" church
that turned out to be shockingly fundamentalist.
It was a place where you were supposed to learn
"mental science", but what you really learned was
that if you were sick and "mental science" couldn't cure you,
it was because you didn't really want to get well. "Mental science"
was infallible, but you were not. There was addiction to a technique,
and there was no compassion in this place. Technique addiction
always squeezes out compassion. The minister bragged
about the sick people she had run off who had failed to benefit
from her "mental science". I now see that she was just too insecure
in her own beliefs, and so couldn't stand to have people around
who might remind her of the shortcomings of those beliefs.

A gentleman spoke up in a class there,
said he'd just quit smoking after four decades on the tobacco weed,
and she immediately disrespected his accomplishment by telling him
that smoking wouldn't hurt him unless he believed it would hurt him.
(Of course, she was a smoker, and in her selfishness was grasping
at this belief so she could continue justifying her own habit . . .
not an honorable behavior pattern from a spiritual "leader".)

Now, that is simplistic thinking, if it can be called thinking at all.
This "mental science" turned out to be not science, but
a form of superstition and dogma. Yes, the very limited method
of this tribe would work sometimes, but no tool is good for
every job. You don't use a drill to saw a tree down, but these folks
used one spiritual tool in trying to meet all their needs. And when
the tool failed, as it frequently did, there was something wrong with
the person. That person failed. That person was bad. If you
have any exposure to any type of fundamentalist religion, that sounds
like a familiar attitude, doesn't it?
Yet this was supposed to be a "New Age" church.
And there are many churches of this particular breed,
teaching their "mental science". I don't know if they
are all fundamentalist or not, but from what I've learned about the religion,
I would not be surprised if they are.

It is said that a little knowledge is a dangerous thing.
This church I briefly attended is the proof of that statement.

Fundamentalism comes about through a pathological desire to be right,
and this extreme desire to be right occurs because the person has
no faith in herself and wants a tried and true method to
cling to. This is ultimately why we have all these
systems in the world for accomplishing various things:
most of us don't trust ourselves to any genuine degree,
so we want something outside of ourselves to trust.
We trust a religion, or an educational system, or a
government beauracracy. We trust a doctor or
a senator or a scientist, instead of learning to trust ourselves.
Well, screw all that. I am here today to
give you some good news: You are trustworthy.
I trust you completely. You are
strong, and you are beautiful,
and you are far superior to any system.
And when you trust your Self
as much as I trust your Self
we'll get along just fine.

TECHNIQUE ADDICTION

Rigidity crushes the life out of you.
Any system or technique
that demands a rigid obedience
or viewpoint will hurt you.
If its methods demand
a rigid application of technique,
sooner or later, it will hurt you.
Flexibility is essential for living life as
the spiritual being that you are.
A system should exist to serve you,
according to how you inform it that you want to be served.

A system is not a Group.
A genuine Group is composed of Souls.
If there is a system in use, it exists so the members of the Group
will have a relatively unified method of implementing
the objectives of the Group, as well as whatever
personal objectives the individual members
may have. The system should have enough grace
to bow out at those times when it cannot
be of service, instead of always trying to
hog the show.

The herd may be addicted to systems,
but a totally conscious Soul will not be.
He may see the beauty and utility of a system,
but it will not rule him.
It will *never* rule him!
He will implement the system in his own way,
if the textbook method doesn't serve
his purposes, and he won't use a system
at all if he doesn't want to.

Any system that thinks it is superior to you
and wants to make you conform to it
is a laughable, infantile system
and it isn't worth your time.
It can be any sort of system:
something for Human Potential,
a martial art,
a government.
Medicine and doctors and Pagan magikal systems.

If a system fails to recognize that YOU
are superior to it,
brush the dirt off your feet
and go find a system
you can use,
instead of one that wants to use you.

BIOGRAPHY OF A TITAN

She is mindless
in a form of primal consciousness
a totally sexual consciousness
wanting only to make the love of passion
and knowing little else.
She has existed forever,
and as a sexual being she
has exhausted her possibilities.
She comes and comes and comes
with the white sea foam of her father
the little "yips" and moans of their sharing
echoing from the cliffs along the shores.
The earth shakes from their lovemaking,
the earth shudders and crashes and screams
energy spurting against energy
energy craving energy and spurting itself
from a mindless race
into a mindless race.
Lathered in foam she waits,
but after all these ages,
she begins to feel insecure.
There must be something more.
But what could it be?

"I am a mother," she breathes
and a daughter.
I make love to the father who created me
and to the son I bore.
This is all I have ever done: made
love to my father and son,
and become swollen with their seed,
and delivered anew of my children.
And made love to my children,
both male and female.
Incest is all I know.

"But if incest is all I know . . .
I can turn it on its head, perhaps
and begin the exploration of myself
to see what else lies within me.
I can channel the energy of the family
more deeply into myself
and know myself more fully

by making love to myself alone for a while.
I will go to a far mountain,
and there I will explore myself
the warm vagina that has known lips
and tongue and tool of my kin,
the bowels of my sweetness,
which may begin again to glisten
with the dawn of a new experience
of all my selves.
And perhaps even of my Self.
I will go now."

She leaves the sea and travels far inland
as far as she can go.
She has crossed deserts
and become a desert
she has crossed the Greenlands
that reminded her of home
and made her laugh brightly.
But only the Greenlands made her laugh,
and she was there only briefly.
Mostly, the trip has been one
of sadness and depression.
There has been no family
to hold to her bosom
for long, long ages
and she misses the lovemaking
of those who were dear to her.
She wishes once more
to take her father inside her chalice
and present him with the special gift
that only she can share with him.
She wishes to sweetly nourish her daughters' and sons'
excited mouths on her rigid nipples
sharing the mother's milk of her desire with them.
Sharing her creamy thighs with them.
For this is all she has ever known.
Until now.
But now, pulled and pushed by the Unknown Force
she travels thru the bowels of experience
and her travails are beyond any of childbirth.
For this time she is the child,
and this time, she is the one being born.

She comes to a village on the slopes of a great mountain,

a volcano. Here reside some of her grandchildren
from long ago. They worship her sweetness in memory,
but do not recognize the dusty hag they see before them.
For the long ages on the road
have thwarted Aphrodite,
and taken her from herself.
No longer vigorous,
or beautiful, or sweet,
they cannot believe she is pure,
but they agree to let her live among them
in a mud hut on the edge of town. Most of
them live in fine straw huts, and a few have grand
homes of logs, but no matter. She will take a
mud hut, and here she will rest a while. Here she
will recover her strength. She hopes.

But no strength comes.
No lover comes to nourish her with
mouth and tongue and rigid meat,
and she is worn and weary.
Once she was called Aphrodite of the Titans,
but now . . .
now they call her nothing, but look away when she approaches.
She is too dry even to weep.
She wishes she could weep.
Sometimes in the flames of her exhaustion and despair,
she calls on the name of her father,
in whose lap she once sat
and whose rigid knowledge filled her
with her own kind of knowing
as she blossomed into womanhood
making him spurt onto his belly,
then laughing and letting him spurt into her chalice.
Bearing sons to him,
and daughters to herself,
sons and daughters that would travel
the wide world and make their way in it,
and who would remember their parents.
Yes, they remember their parents,
but Aphrodite has changed beyond their recognition.
She touches the leathery vagina, in desperation
she offers herself to the people in the town square,
but they laugh at her and pelt her with fruit. She is
decadent, greedily she eats the fruit as her grandchildren
laugh and point and jeer at the naked old grandmother

who believes she is Aphrodite. "If you are Aphrodite,"
they hoot, "make yourself young and beautiful again,
and we will come unto you to love you, and be your
grandchildren."

But she bleeds from wounds in her hands
and feet, and it is not her destiny to cater
to the illusions of those who promote suffering.
She suffers alone. She will never respond
to her degenerate heirs who promote suffering.

The mayor rapes her. He approaches her
in the town square as she greedily
gobbles the fruit they'd pelted her with.
"Sweet Aphrodite," he sneers, "I have some
fruit for sweet Aphrodite. Toothless old hag,
imposter, don't you realize it's a felony
to impersonate a goddess? We believe
in our laws. You must be disciplined."
He pulls out his rigid meat, the meat that had
known passion many times, but never love.
A petty king, ruled by his own scepter.

He approaches her from behind, and
like a dog he mounts her.
She hadn't been penetrated in so many years,
and now the desolate pole of the enforcer
tore its way into the depths of her cunt,
tearing and burning all the way past
her belly. She felt it, felt it go
way, way inside her, and there was nothing she
could do. She writhed and squirmed in his
hands, but he only laughed and
shoved more harshly. He laughed,
and the townsfolk laughed with him.
Then he panted and panted, and moaned as she squirmed,
and then he screamed in rage as he shot her full
of his filthy gray creme.
The townsfolk laughed.
A couple of small boys
took the mark of the mayor,
asked him to make the mark
of his name for them on a clay
tablet. He did so,
breathing heavily and smirking, huge cock

still half-hard for all to see.
The boys thanked the mayor and ran off,
happy to carry something of their idol's with them.

The mayor went around to the front of Aphrodite,
stood in front of her as she cowered miserably.
He slapped her in the face
with his cock, then again. And again.
He felt that one more slap might kill her,
so he stopped. She'd only committed
a minor felony, after all.

"Toothless bitch, don't commit sacrilege again.
It is blasphemy to pretend to be a goddess.
You're nothing but a sick old whore.
I don't want to have to fuck you again
in front of the whole town, so don't commit any more
crimes. You say you love us? Hah! Well, bitch, we
don't love you. You're not our goddess. You're just
some old straggler who wandered into town. We
never should have given you a cup of water,
let alone allowed you to live in that old hut.
Now you've got a record, we know what you are.
All we have to do is look at your record and see you've
committed a felony. You're a criminal, so wear the
brand. You'll get no special treatment from us.
Goddess? Bullshit."

He stormed off, leaving her
dripping blood and the leavings of his semen
from her ravaged vagina. She sobbed
a little, but no tears would come.
She was as dry as a bone.
Seemed like she'd been that way forever.
Dry as a bone.

Aphrodite lay in her hut.
There was no food,
but it rained often enough
so she had water.
She collected it in a dish and drank it down.
She was bruised and hurting from the rape of
the enforcer of laws, and she lay
for a long time in her hut
without food. A deer came to her then,

fleet of foot and sharp of instinct. No
hunter had ever been able to apprehend
this deer, the most cunning buck of
the forest. He lay down beside her,
and said: "Goddess Aphrodite, those of us
who recognize ourselves as part of Nature
still adore you. We worship you and sing praises to
you. But these offspring of the gods,
these mortal men and women,
have forgotten both their Divine origin
and Nature. They live in a souless place
without merit in the order of things, neither of
one kingdom or the other, though partaking
of both. They must be led . . ."

"Sweet buck," Aphrodite rasped, "I cannot
lead those who forsake me. I don't
even fully know myself yet, how could I lead
even if they would accept me? But they
will not accept me, that much is plain."

"It has come to the attention of the company of animals,"
said the buck carefully, "that you are with child,
Goddess Aphrodite. You carry the child of him who raped
you, the child of the enforcer of the laws of man.
It is your duty to give birth to this child, and perhaps in the
giving you will learn enough about yourself
to be of service in the world of men."

He surveyed her critically.   "In any case,
a Goddess deserves a sacrifice, so I
have come to sacrifice myself to you.
You are hungry. Kill and eat."

"No . . ." she began, but was suddenly
seized with the urgency of an
unknown prompting from her womb,
and she fell upon the buck and slew him
with her knife.

He smiled as he died. "Thank you,
my Goddess," he whispered.

With trembling hands, Aphrodite
followed the pattern she had seen

the village butcher perform,
and she butchered her wild friend,
and that night she dined on him.
She cut him up into strips
and dried him in the sun
so that the meat would last,
and he nourished her for a long time.

Autumn came amid the roaring of the winds.
A wail was heard from the mud hut,
a wailing from the miserable old woman
who believed she was a goddess.
The townsfolk crossed themselves
for protection and moved quickly
past her hut. They were growing
more uncomfortable with her,
and many believed she was a
witch. They were considering making
witchcraft a felony punishable by death.
They had to do *some*thing. Who
knew what that old woman might do?

A wailing . . . Aphrodite, who had given
birth so many times in her former life,
screamed with the agony of the new life
that was coming out of her as she delivered
herself of child. He walked
from the moment of his birth.
He would not be held by
his mother, but walked on wobbly
legs to the door,
peering up into the sky as
though searching for the sun.
But there was no sun;
the day was cloudy and it would be an
early winter. He looked back
at the old bleeding, suffering hag
who was his mother as if to say,
"I will bring you the sun, Mother.
One day, the sun will be yours."

Then he wobbled back to her
and they embraced one another
and he fell asleep in her arms.

Seasons passed. Apollo--for that was the name
her son had chosen for himself--sported
in the trees, trying to catch the sun.
And the sun always came out for him. He
would climb the wild grapevines
into the tops of the trees and seat himself
in a great fork, or upon a long branch,
and he would whirl with the wind and
shout, and he would glow golden with
the sun, whose child he was. Aphrodite saw
that although the mayor had donated his seed,
the young sapling she had borne was really somehow
the son of the sun. He left his roots
and was absorbed into the sun each day,
it seemed. Sometimes she couldn't
tell Apollo from the sun at all,
there seemed no difference.
He was the son of the sun,
and of all those she had borne
over countless millennia,
he shone the brightest.

The townsfolk still feared Aphrodite,
but for a different reason.
They saw that Apollo,
though still a boy,
was perfectly capable of defending
his mother,
and that he had a natural skill
with all kinds of weapons.
A great bird who lived in a lava cave
on the mountain had taught the boy
all kinds of "tricks", as the townsfolk
put it. The bird was self-sufficient
and never descended into the town,
and the townsfolk had always been content
to leave him to his devices deep in his
lava cave. Truth be told, they
were afraid to go after him to
"bring him to justice", even after
they came up with an infraction
to charge him with. Well,
nobody wants to fight a bird that big,
and certainly not one who is well armed.
For the bird was a master of every weapon,

as well as of unarmed combat,
and he had taught the boy these skills.
The bird was a lover of the sun,
and he enjoyed passing on his skills
to the son of the sun.
The bird's name was Horace.

"Apollo," his mentor said one day, "you must
understand that you are greater than restriction.
To restrict someone is to commit a crime
against nature, and to restrict yourself
is to commit a crime against yourself.
Restriction is not the same thing as
discipline. We discipline ourselves here
on this lava plain, we refine ourselves into
warriors; me because it has always been
my custom, and you so your can defend your
mother.

"We are disciplined, but we are not restrained.
Pardon my French, but I do not give a
rat's ass what those little folk down in the town
believe. They suffer from low self-esteem,
which means they lack the confidence to begin
a program of personal refinement, or to
stick with it even if they started. So instead
of embracing discipline and imposing the rhythm
of their own souls onto their lives, they live in
a hemmed-in, restrained fashion. Everything
they do is based on restriction rather than expansion.
Only a truly disciplined person can expand with his
soul, but they restrict themselves away from
contact with their souls. They are perverse.
They do not love, for love cannot penetrate restriction."

Apollo's brow furrowed. "Then restriction is the shell of discipline.
Restriction is what you have left
if you remove the life from discipline.
Restriction is an empty procedure
created by those whose outlook is devoid of life.
We must destroy the systems
of the world, for they are based on restriction.
They are without love, and they turn the people
into oxen."

Horace cleared his throat delicately. "Not 'we', Apollo.
I've served my time
and I'm in retirement now.
You can do whatever picks your cotton,
but I'm staying put on this mountain."

"Well, all right then, big bird.
You have to follow your heart,
as I must follow mine. But
right now my heart is with my mother,
so with her I will remain. If I
destroy the world, it will only be
after I am certain my mother is
well cared for."

Horace shrugged. Really, Apollo
reminded himself of himself when he was
younger and flying like a swift buzzard
over the desert. He used to fly as high
as he could and try to touch the sun, and a
couple of times he got his wings singed. And
he changed the world, too, though the
changing brought him nothing but heartache.
Now he cherished his retirement.
He was one old buzzard who was content
to remain on his mountain.

More seasons passed, and Apollo
came to mastership in the art of warriorship.
He bested Horace one day,
and the old bird momentarily looked undignified
amidst his flying feathers.
But then he laughed,
and awarded Apollo his shield,
and his sword.
"I believe you will also find
a use for these items," Horace
chuckled, and handed Apollo a
shining golden helmet
and a spear.
"Whosoever lets fly with this spear
while wearing this helmet
will always strike the mark,
at least as long as they are sober.
It usually works when they are drunk, too."

Apollo gathered these items to himself,
grateful to the old bird who
had been his friend all the years
of his life. "I will miss you, Horace,"
he said, knowing the old bird
wanted to sleep, and that he
would not be seen for a very long time.

"You will find me in your heart,
Apollo. And we will
dream of one another,
whenever it is convenient,
or when necessity arises. For
teammates must always stand ready
to assist one another, whether awake or asleep.
Thus the team itself grows.
Goodnight, sweet friend.
Take care of your mother for me. She
and I knew one another long ago,
when giants roamed the earth.
She is no longer the same woman,
but this is no tragedy. All beings
must grow, all beings must follow the law
of change. A period of decadence
sometimes precedes change. Your
decadent mother, so dry and lifeless,
still has a spark in her heart. *YOU*
are that spark, Apollo. You
have provided the spark
that kept her alive the last
eighteen years, and now you must
show her how the spark
can become the flame of
purification and alter
the gross matter she has
allowed herself to fall into.
She must be shown the way
of the truly pure,
abandoning ancient ways
that no longer serve."

"I will suceed, Horace."

"I know you will, my friend."
They embraced, and Horace looked at

the sun once more, and at the son
of the sun whom he had come to love.
Then with a smile, as though
a great burden had been lifted,
Horace leapt into the sky and vanished.

Aphrodite had not been well.
She had done her best to hide
her condition from Apollo,
but she knew she was not long for this world.
Aphrodite of the Titans had fallen so low . . .
she wondered about her father,
and her brothers and sisters whom she also mothered,
her divine offspring
that came about thru the lovemaking she shared
with her father and sons
in the great cyclic wheel of all Creation.

Creation . . .
but there was no more Creation,
she mused sadly. All
was in disarray.
If her father and her brothers and sisters
and the sons and daughters
whom she bore to her father and brothers
still lived at all, it must be in some
remote place, and perhaps they
were as decadent and decayed and lonely as she was.
No one mentioned the Titans anymore.

Apollo stood in the doorway of the mud hut
and Aphrodite brightened, as always she did
in his presence. He shined upon her with a
splendid glory, and in those times
when he was at home, instead of up
on the mountain training, she loved him
so brightly in her heart that the radiance
remained for days after he went back to the
mountain. She touched her hair,
ashamed of her decadence, yet with
a bright spark glowing thru
the shame.

"Apollo, my son," she croaked, trying
unsuccessfully to arise from the straw pallet

where she lay for days at a time,
too weak to even feed herself,
or to bathe.
"Apollo . . ."

"I am here, my blessed Mother, she
who bore me with no regard
for anything but love. Mother,
you could have abandoned me,
but you chose to try to know me,
and to help me live so I could know
myself.
I have learned much from being with Horace,
and he and you together gave me the space
I needed to understand myself,
and to come into the fulness of my manhood.
Now I am a man."

Aphrodite whimpered, joy mixed with melancholy. For
her dream for her son had been realized,
but now she knew she must die. She
had exceeded what she believed was the
limit of her endurance many, many times,
yet she had always survived for her son.
Apollo had needed her to survive,
but now he was a man. Now
she would go to her rest . . .

Apollo approached the filthy straw pallet,
saddened that his mother had had to
live in such filth. But he knew
there had been no way around it. Still,
he could make her final moments easier
and help with the translation that she would undergo.
He vowed that with his help,
Aphrodite's translation would be a success.

"Let me make you easy, Mother."
Apollo leaned down and kissed her,
then took her arm and helped her
to her feet. He led her
into the warm sunlight that streamed in
from the door.
They stood in the sunlight
streaming in from the door.

Then Apollo led Aphrodite into the warm,
into the warm sweet green grasses,
into the warmth of the embrace
of nature, with all her buzzing insects
and odours of delight. She had
not seen these things for a long time.

Apollo, shield on his left arm
and sword in its scabbard
held Aphrodite on his right arm
as he studied nature and his place in it.
He felt quickened, and the fire in his
loins turned to gold. Something
good was going on.

His helmet was on his head,
the spear in the hand
of the arm that supported his mother.
Aphrodite felt quickened, too, and
for the first time in untold ages glanced
shyly at a man, the young warrior at
her side. She reached out
as though to touch the sharp edge
of the head of the spear, then drew back
as her fingers flew to her mouth. The
spear was sharp and would cut. It
was a man's tool.

Aphrodite had never wielded
a man's tool. In all the warm
ages of her life, all her radiance
had come from the gentle dance done by
a woman of gentle heart and flowing
passion as she seeks to spread
happiness and healing and love.
She had always sought to spread love.
The implements of battle she left
to her father and brothers,
that was where their interest lay.
She'd only wanted to love them and cleanse
them when they returned from a new adventure.

She felt light inside as she reflected
that her son was as her father and brothers
had been so long ago . . . yes, he was

like them, but he was very different, too.
No one, not even the Titans Themselves,
remembered being anything other than
what they were. They were as they'd
always been, springing forth from
Aphrodite and her daughters as fixed agents,
never needing refinement . . . or perhaps
just never wanting the bother of it.
But Apollo . . . yes, she reflected, this
one was different, indeed. He had
spent eighteen years on the mountain
purifying himself, becoming more and
more refined, more and more able to
reflect the light of the sun. And
now that work was finished, and he stood
beside her a true man, one who
had created himself. Yes, he was self-created.
That is how he was different from her father
and brothers and daughters and her wives.
He was self-created, and he shone like
a great golden lion, supreme and unafraid.
There had been many times of weakness
in his life, times when the rigors of his path
threatned to burst apart the steaming
cauldron of his life, but he had
dealt with these challenges as a man of
great courage, and ultimately survived
and won the day.
The result stood besider her now,
and she leaned on his arm
and began to reflect a little bit
of the warmth back onto him.
Apollo, the self-created,
looked down upon her and smiled.

He drew her to him,
and together they walked to the blue
river, to an emerald patch of
grass that helped frame
the blue river. He sat her down
beneath a tree that was heavy laden
with fruit, and he removed his sword
and his shield and his helmet.
He leaned the great spear
against the tree.

The grass was thick and soft,
and it cushioned Aphrodite as she lay upon it.
She sighed, wishing she'd had the strength
to get to the river more often. "Oooh . . ."
she stretched her bent old frame a little,
and her legs parted enough to stretch
her most sacred region . . . the most
sacred region second only to the heart,
and she remembered all the floodings
of her heart into her sacred chalice
when she was young. But now
she was old and ashamed. She was dying . . .
yet in the dying she was feeling the old glow
again, not intensely, but percolating . . .
suddenly she gasped as her nipples became hard,
she'd forgotten how that felt.
Yet she was an old woman
and today she would die.

Suddenly she noticed that Apollo
was studying her as though he were
reading her mind. He smiled.
"You have nothing to be ashamed of, Mother.
You have done your duty. You are a
Titan. You have lived as a Titan,
and you will die as a Titan, always
being true to your heart and to your duty.
But even Titans have to rest, Mother.
Even you have to rest.
You have contributed to the world,
and you have contributed to me.
You have earned the right to be translated.
A new day will soon dawn upon the earth,
and you must be translated."

Her gnarled hand drew the tattered fabric
of her dress across her bosom,
and the fabric dragged the nipples
and made them sing as
a little whimper escaped her throat.
She did not have to be ashamed of
being old. She had followed her heart,
and it had led to this river, and all
was right with the world.
She felt a touch of the old

confidence begin to return,
and she smiled at Apollo,
as he smiled back at her.

Apollo plucked some fruit
and sat down next to his mother.
She lay there, and he rested her
head in his lap. He chewed some
fruit, and it was the delicious fruit
that sometimes comes to a man
and a woman who have begun to
know themselves. He felt his insides
begin to rejoice, and he took some
of the fruit he had chewed from his
mouth and offered it to Aphrodite,
for she no longer had the teeth
to chew her own food.

Aphrodite licked the fruit from
Apollo's fingers, suddenly growing
stronger and feeling the fruit quicken her
with the knowledge of what the future
might hold. For the future was dear;
Apollo walked in the future, and
anyplace Apollo walked was dear.
She swallowed the fruit as its
juices ran down her cheeks,
and she slowly sucked the juices
from the fingers of her son.
Her son grew tight with a certain longing.

Apollo saw a certain beauty in Aphrodite
he'd never seen before. The old mother
who bore new life had always seemed
beautiful to his heart, but never to
his loins. But now he knew a certain
potential in her; he saw both her past
glory among the family of the Titans
and the future that might be.
He found that his fingers were tracking
across her bodice, and he
began to marvel, for he had never
touched a woman in this way before.
The hard nipples caused his hands to
cramp with desire as he caressed her,

this old woman who lay with her
head in his lap and her legs slightly parted.

Aphrodite moaned . . . a look of zeal
began to overcome her as she began to sweat.
What was happening . . . oooh! She hadn't felt
this way in so many years, and had never
expected to feel this desire again, or the touch of
a man. Certainly she had never expected
to become intimate in this fashion with her son,
him who thought only of training to protect her
and keep her from harm.
She felt her tongue, moist with desire,
slide around her lips, and she reached
almost frantically for Apollo . . .

Apollo shifted his position and lay down
next to his mother, beneath the great
fruit tree that exemplified their knowledge.
But the tree also contained life,
and life more abundantly.
The tree was the Tree of Forever,
and those who tasted its fruit
would know themselves well and would
be elevated into the true race of Immortals.

So Apollo lay with Aphrodite and they
looked into one another's eyes. Suddenly
they laughed with joy. In her whole
life, Aphrodite had never felt anything
more grand than the tender sweetness
of this moment. Something of
her more youthful self came over her,
and she grinned and turned into Apollo,
and wrapped him in her arms and in
her love. She pulled him to her,
and today would be an initiation for them both.
Her hand upon his cheek, she gazed with mirth
into his eyes, and saw that he had her eyes. Why
hadn't she noticed that before?
She felt his tender heart begin to beat
according to his true nature, and she
saw that the true nature of everything
is LOVE.
So she giggled and continued.

She turned her lips onto his
and felt refreshed as the drink of
her son's energy poured through her.
His breath sang a song all the way
though her as she drank of him.

As they taught one another,
Apollo lay there sucking on her tongue,
the tongue that had nourished so many men
in ancient times. Her tongue slid in and out
between his teeth, and he sucked on it
in a frenzy, never wanting to be without it.

Apollo began to return the kiss . . .
then the eagerness seized him
and he drove his tongue into her,
and in all his days he'd never driven
a javelin more eagerly than this.
He drove his tongue into her as she
sucked with joy upon it,
for each so enjoyed sucking on the other's tongue.
To suck the tongue of a loved one
is an act of supreme devotion and sharing.

Her leg pressed against his swollen manhood,
that part of him that had never known woman
and which ached for expression.
He embraced her with such a strength
he might have shattered her bones,
but neither of them cared.
They were locked into one another,
and an eternity might pass and
they would never know it,
for they were already lost in eternity,
and never wished to be anyplace else.
The mother and the son swam with
one another in eternity,
and as long as their loving continued
no tragedy could befall the universe
or her children.

There was a roaring in Apollo's ears . . .
and over the roaring, a chorus
like a host of joyful angels
as he penetrated the mysteries of his mother.

They were naked now, and
he put himself inside her where he
had always belonged. They gazed
clearly upon one another's souls,
and neither was afraid.
Neither of them would ever be afraid again.

Apollo pushed and pushed, deeper into her,
deeper into the knowing of his mother,
deeper into her dark mysteries,
the mysteries that veiled the light of her heart.
For no heart can ever be seen by the unworthy.
Only the self-created can truly know the heart.
Apollo created himself anew with each
gasping breath he took as he lay with his mother.
Apollo had believed he was self-created before,
but now he saw that there are degrees of
self-creation. Now he felt
born anew and cleansed. Now he
felt born in a truer sense.
Apollo expanded, and he felt bigger
than he ever had before.

He screamed . . . he was a Void,
and the Void that he was
screamed in his ears as the essence
of all Creation spurted out of him
into the sweet warm Chalice
that had been provided for it.

He blinked out of existence.

Suddenly, there were stars, and he
was a star, and his mother was a star.
Every being in all Creation was a star.
The ladybug on the leaf was a star.
Each bird was a star, each singing
the song of the stars.

The stars sang all around him,
the human stars,
the stars called Titans long ago,
the stars that would be the
humans of the future. He
saw them all, and he loved them

all, for he loved himself. There
are no distinctions between one star
and another star.

For a long time,
Apollo just lay there among the stars.

Then he slept.

He awoke, feeling that every
thirst he had ever had had
been filled. He would never
be thirsty again.
He lay there with his eyes closed,
rejoicing sweetly at the light
he could feel radiating at him
from some nearby star.
He could even see the picture
of its light on his closed eyelids.
He was so happy!

But finally he had to stir.
So he began to sit up . . .

And found a woman sitting on his stomach.
She was naked, and she sat on him
just above the region of his
newly awakened manhood.
It doesn't get much better than this, Apollo reflected.

She was a young woman, with
golden skin and blonde hair so
light it was platinum.
She was as beautiful as Aphrodite
had been reputed to be in her youth,
but he could tell she wasn't Aphrodite.
Aphrodite was all softness, but this woman . . .
this woman was strong. Young
she might be, but she radiated an
inner strength and power
that practically stunned Apollo.
He had no idea what to say
to such a powerful being,
but he said the first thing
that popped into his head:

"Happy Birthday!"

The young lady cocked her head,
her expression indicating a distaste for nonsense.
But then she shrugged. "Yes, it's my
eighteenth birthday, now that
you mention it. For a moment
I'd forgotten. I've had some
pretty strange dreams today
and I'm still trying to make sense
out of them."

"I understand," he said. "Here,
let me get up."

She swung her leg over him
and dismounted, bracing with her hand
on his stomach. The touch of this woman . . .
Apollo had never felt so warm,
even after a twenty-mile run in full armour
with Horace flying above his head
threatening to shit on him if he stopped.

They faced one another on their knees
and suddenly both of them smiled.
Then they broke out into laughter,
and slapped their palms together
and locked fingers.
Laughing, laughing.

After a bit they embraced.
It was a long embrace,
and for the second time that day
Apollo's manhood was quickened.
She guided him into her,
and there he stayed for some time,
fully conscious of both flesh
and of eternity. He had not
believed it was possible to be
conscious of both at once,
but now he saw that it was.
And he was glad.

Both Apollo and the powerful young woman
in his arms saw that there was no better

medium for Divinity to know Itself
than thru a human being. All
human beings were gods and goddesses,
and all were eternal and temporal.
Most humans only saw the temporal part,
but the self-created humans, those who
had chosen to do the work to become Immortals,
saw both at once. To be a fully
conscious human being is to be
everything in the universe
and be aware that you are
everything in the universe.
You are also the Void.

They stayed locked in a soft bliss for some time.
Then Apollo turned her face to his. He saw
himself swimming in her eyes.
"What name will you choose for
yourself, beautiful lady?"

"I have already chosen, Apollo. I am
called Athena, and I will walk the
earth with you."

Apollo's heart expanded a little more. "Athena . . . yes.
A powerful name for a powerful woman.
A name to incite worship, for you are
beautiful and strong, and you are
my equal in all things."

She smiled, just a little. She pulled
him out of her gently,
and held his beautiful manhood
tenderly for a moment.
Then they stood together.

She spoke. "The old ways have
vanished, Apollo. The old world
has been washed away. Both
men and gods must adapt,
even as the physical surface
of the earth adapts. I am
happy that it is so. We Immortals
do not fear change, we welcome it.
We use change as a medium to express

ourselves, to know ourselves. For
us, change is a medium of Art.
Every Immortal is the Artist of his Life,
and of his Lives. It is only the
mortal men and women who fear
change, for they've never gotten
to know themselves as
citizens of eternity. But for
the Self-Created, change is a
mother's milk."

Apollo got dressed,
sliding his sword into its scabbard
and picking up his shield.
"We'll have to find you some clothes
before winter," he observed,
still looking at Athena with
great pleasure.

She laughed, tossing back her hair.
"That is so. But for now, this
spear and helmet lying here will
be sufficient. I believe I
can make good use of these tools
in the world of mortal men and women."

She picked up the helmet and put it on,
then grasped and hefted the spear
with a little gasp of pleasure.
"I'll be quite a marksman with this.
I'll be able to reveal truth in a way
Aphrodite never could,
for all her glory and flexibility.
Now that we've begun to know one
another, Apollo, we've achieved a
powerful integration."

"Yes, sweetheart," Apollo responded,
knowing he had a partner to ride
the river with.

ELITISM NEVER LASTS

Brutal, dirty. A philosophy that debases,
and tries to force itself upon reality,
the reality of human suffering.
Human nature is not subject
to any philosophy; the best
any philosophy can hope for is to
complement human nature,
not replace it. But the
brutal, dirty intellectuals of
the right promote their glamour,
the glamour of commerce and the
enslavement of the factory, and
they abuse the intellect to justify
their schemes to abuse humanity.
All for what they consider to be a profit.
But is it really profit, when you doom
yourself to being exploited in a future life
for the pain you have caused others
in your present life?

When the drug companies play their little
games to deny medicine to those who
can't pay . . . can it be that anyone
who is truly a human being
would engage in such behavior?
No, such behavior is impossible from a
human being. They are not human. Not
yet. After they have profited enough,
reaping their reward of agony in enough
lifetimes, then they will decide they
want to become human. Then
they will learn to embrace
compassion, and manifest it in service
to humanity, forgetting about "profit".
But they are not there yet. They
are not human beings.
They currently are beasts,
manifesting a dirty cunning.
They are in hell.
That is why they deserve our compassion.

TWISTED

She is twisted, a liberal
playing right into the hands
of the drug companies,
and other unfortunate enterprises that
crush the human soul in their mad
quest for profits.
She believes in judgments and categories.
She believes in the dotted line, and
in the fine print,
and in a multitude of qualifications.
The suffering doesn't matter to her. All
she cares about is whether she should
check this box or that box. Her
objective is to check boxes, not eliminate
human suffering. Maybe she's just weak . . .

No sane person can believe
that a person who is in agony
and has no money to pay to the
exploiters for their insurance coverage,
and who cannot work . . .
no sane or compassionate human being
can believe that such a person should not be
served. If Jesus or Buddha or Socrates
had had that attitude, then
where would we be?
Are *you* spiritually aware,
or do you require someone else to come into the earth,
to ground spiritual energies you haven't
learned to handle? Do you think
that the people who are responsible
for grounding these spiritual energies
ever charge for the service?
No, they never charge. It is
a free service they provide to you
because they love you. They want
you to have your chance
to begin to grow as a spiritual being.
It seems to me that the least *you* could do,
would be to help insure the physical survival of your
fellow citizens, even when they don't
have any money to give you, and that you could do it
without charging them the price of their

dignity and reducing their lives to a petty little formula.
The objective, after all, is to eliminate suffering,
not use a bureaucracy to add to it.
If you can't do that much,
you haven't learned even a little bit
about tapping into the spiritual energies
that have been grounded for you
by people who never charged you
for doing what you could never
have done for yourself.

Therefore, you are a spoiled baby.

STICK OF STOVE WOOD

I got knocked in the head with
a stick of stove wood.
That's a pretty rough metaphor
for a pretty rough life.
But I needed to become tender,
and now I have.
The stick of stove wood
was my salvation.

ZEN POESY

If'n you don't watch whut you're doin',
doggie dog, you gonna create some
bad karma, bub. You is.

Doggie Dog pants to himself . . .
confused, seeking the clear light.
Forlorn.
Breakfast,
then squash and beans
at noon.
Fearful,
can't see the clear light yet.
Wait! (Pants excitedly)
He'll see it on his deathbead. Now
everything's fine.

Yes, suh, doggie dog. Wait 'till your
deathbead. See that clear light then.
Forget about now, now you got's to
manage folks and make a profit.

"Doggie Dog, wake up! Wake up, man!"

"Furry Kitten, is that you?"

"It's me. I thought you were dead . . ."

"Damn near was dead, Furry Kitten. Glad you
came along."

QUEER YEAR

It's been a queer year
a pretty queer year
and I'm not even gay.
No pink triangles for me,
and I will not fellate thee.
But still, it's been a pretty queer year.

Observations from the controllers
they said rightly
that I cannot be controlled.
They also said rightly
that I am sane.
I am the first sane person
they've ever met
who cannot be controlled.
But surely there must
be more like me.
As we increase,
I am sure
we will make the controllers nervous.

More queer years to come . . .
queer years for the controllers, that is.
I'm just going to follow my bliss
and see where that leads.

SELFHOOD

Don't be controlled by anything,
including your own philosophy,
for a philosophy without YOU in the center
is a dead philosophy.
YOU are the engine,
the lifeforce, that motivates a
doctrine, and YOU are superior
to the doctrine.
There will be times when the doctrine
will not apply, no matter how sound
it generally is. Go with
the energy, baby. Go with
your SELF, don't allow your
SELF to become depleted by some
usurping doctrine. That doctrine
which usurps must be replaced by
one that compliments.

Don't be controlled by anything,
including your own philosophy.
You must decide whether to be
a trained animal, or perhaps a computer,
or perhaps a human being. The
human beings of the future
will be uncontrollable.
They will be highly disciplined,
but they will be uncontrollable.
Do you want to be one of them?
Then get started today.
Their philosophy is superior,
and it compliments them.
They rule their own philosophy
and submit themselves to the ENERGY
which they in fact are.

ENERGY is where it's at, baby.
ENERGY is what we are.
We can channel a little of
our SELF into a philosophy,
but we are just too big
for a philosophy to contain us.
There is more than our philosophy,
and there is more than the philosophy

of the future humans.
There is SELFHOOD.

WOULD JESUS HAVE BEEN A LAWYER?

A penis in her mouth
she lies like a rotting corpse
because degenerate Christianity told her
she had to lie like a rotting corpse
and be ashamed
and not enjoy herself.

The second penis,
in her vagina,
ravages her with all the passion
the dead reserve for one another.
Cold passion of Christian fear
spurting out upon her, into her, upon her
coating her with Christian lust.
Where's the Christian love?
Not in those who use her
and not in those who tell her
she should be ashamed to let
herself be used.

The Sacred Prostitutes of old
used to enjoy performing their
healing services. Sexuality is
the biggest part of the biological and emotional human,
so without directly touching and addressing
and licking and sucking
on the sexual, there can be no true healing.
But Christianity removed the sacred
from life on earth.
Christianity removed the sacred from
her life.
She thinks of herself as a whore,
instead of joyfully wearing the
title of Prostitute.
If she were a Prostitute
instead of a furtive whore,
she wouldn't have a drug habit
to support
and would have an excess of all abundance.
She could then volunteer
some of her services to the community.
Perhaps demonstrate sexuality
on the village green,

or in the high school classroom
with some of her liberated friends.
But today's prostitute doesn't see herself
as holy, all because of the chains
of degenerate Christianity.
You would think
that the degenerate Christians would see
they are hurting themselves worst of all
by their assault on tenderness. People
in remote times, barbaric as they were,
would never have been so insane.
Christians are insane,
and they lack compassion.
They have forgotten Jesus.

She charges her usual fee
and smiles (faked that, too)
before going out to scout
for another good Christian
who will pay for her services.

CHRISTIAN LIFE
AND MUSLIM, AND JEWISH

They deny psychology
and their psyche bites them on the bum.
Everything they deny rears its ugly
head, the head that only became
ugly when they first repressed it.
Now it seeks appeasement. It
knows they will not embrace it, but--
perhaps they will turn it loose for a
few minutes at a time,
like some half-tamed dog
that has spent most of its life
in a little bitty pen.

MOTIVES

A perverted appetite requires
forbidden fruit.
Christianity has never been able
to eliminate prostitution.
It has only been able to
create sluts and whores
out of a class of royalty.

A PROSTITUTE'S HEART

There is a reason we have the American myth
of the prostitute with the heart of gold.
The *real* prostitute does have a heart of gold,
and gives of herself, bestowing healing upon others
by the grace of her presence.

There aren't many of these women
left in America, but by the grace
of the Goddess, they shall arise again.

Actually, a few of them are already arising,
and over time more will come.
They know that life is about
more than a stiff member.
They also know that sometimes a stiff member
can serve as the gateway to the heart.
They are good, and they help to spread
the energy of GOD.
They serve GODDESS, and whosoever serves GODDESS
also serves GOD.

MY INTERNAL LANDSCAPE

I kiss the foot of Athena,
she who inspires me,
and I kiss Aphrodite's foot
for she propels my loins,
and that can be quite an inspiration
in itself.

I see crosses on a hill,
lots more than three of them.
And I have been crucified
on each one.
Each one bears years of
my bloodstains.
At least I got my tetanus shot,
and I guess it worked.

It has occurred to me
that my internal landscape
may seem pretty unique
to some folks.
But to me every day
is just another day
replete with goblins
and crucifixions
and wonderful Prostitutes
who tell me bedtime stories.
Some days I am nourished,
others . . . I don't want
to talk about the others.
If thoughts are things,
I'd rather think about the things
I want to experience
so that maybe tomorrow
will be a day of Athena
or of Aphrodite,
or one of their younger sisters
who has only been incarnate
for two or three decades.
To put me in a good humour,
all it would really take would be
the outworking of the energy
I have grounded in this incarnation.
Freedom, Love, Will, and Intelligence

would appear on earth,
and I could go home.

After one more dalliance with
a Sacred Prostitute, of course!

PETALUMA

Petaluma KOA
another stop along the way.
Pretty big town
with the traffic all headed down
to San Francisco.

Goats and sheep
across a fence
a pastoral scene.
I'm living out of
the bed of my truck.
California's this way,
rural and city mixed.
Pretty interesting,
the combinations you run into.
Sebastopol seemed more urban
than Petaluma, despite being smaller
and farther from San Francisco.

Quail running around everywhere.
Blacktail deer not too
far away.
City deer, city quail.
They have hair,
and feathers.
I have a truck.

I have a truck . . .
been driving this old truck
for seven years, and I'll
be driving it lots more years,
until well after the turn of
the century. Right
now it's 1995.

Strange . . . I did a report
on Petaluma in college. I'm
talking to a girl about that,
and I find out Petaluma's changed.
They dropped the ordinance I wrote
about in my report. I thought
it was a pretty good ordinance.
But that's the way people are,

I guess. Drop the few good
laws, so they'll have more room
for bad laws.

I am fascinated by Petaluma,
even though I only stay one
night in this campground,
then proceed on my way.
The energy here is of
interest to me. I don't
know how to qualify it,
but I am fascinated by
the energy of the place.
Almost like a cowtown,
yet with all the amenities,
and then some. Caught
between sophisticated
Sebastopol and the shining
of the Golden Gate,
this California town is
almost like a third breast.
It is the big breast in the middle,
and it is full of milk.

CALIFORNIA COAST

Grey cliffs, and medium mountains
and the breaking of the surf.
This isn't like Florida at all.
No flat country in these parts.
Mendocino . . . a strange little jewel.
Bet it costs two fortunes
to live here, but at
least the tourists seem
to have a good time.
Ft. Bragg--there's one
on each coast--nice town,
but I don't see any military
installation in this California burg.
Bodega Bay . . . damn,
that big fish head scared the hell
out of me! What is that . . .
almost like a big catfish head
mounted on the wall, but I
think it's a sturgeon. Well,
I guess it's the master of
its domain, since this *is* a
seafood restaurant.

The Northern California coast
must be a quail hunter's paradise.
Quail running around everywhere,
and they even have elk
a little farther north.
Ukiah . . . Boonville . . .
inland towns with history
and glory, and a river
called the Russian.
The Russians were all over
this part of California in
pioneer days, left their mark.
Bodega Bay, Sebastopol . . .
Russian influence in the naming of towns.

FT. BENNING AND COLUMBUS, GA.

"Show us your tits, bitch!" my
buddy Clyde yells. His manner
becomes more insulting after
she leaves the stage, and she
knocks the hell out of her lover when
he tries to prevent her from knocking
the hell out of Clyde. Damn, Clyde!
These girls have a hard way to go;
be nice to them, old buddy. It's
okay to get drunk and slobber
on their sweet titties, but at
least do it respectfully. Say
sweet things to the sweet ladies,
don't insult them.

But Clyde continues, and soon
he is bounced out of the place,
along with some more of my buddies.
I am drunk as ten skunks, but I
have respected strippers from
the first moment I ever laid eyes on one,
and I would not deliberately do anything
to cause them distress. Yes, I slobber on
them as much as anyone, and more than most,
since they give me free dances and sit
beside me and upon my lap, but
my drunkenness is a respectful
drunkenness. You have to
be respectful when you go to church,
and this strip joint is my church. It is
my temple, and the ladies are my priestesses.

When we come in from the field,
cammoed up and nasty,
the first thing we want to do
is eat a decent meal, then go
to the stripper church. We get
drunk there and we worship.
Well, I worship. The other guys
wonder why I'm the one
who gets all the free dances.
I guess I'm just an altarboy,
and the freebies of touch

and tongue I receive
are the fringe benefits
of my service
to my beautiful friends.

ROOT II

Behold!
His name is Root,
and he standeth before you.
Thine eyes be wide, lass.
Hast thou never seen such?
No? Then sport
with Root for a while.
He feels good about you,
and he'll feel good inside you, too.
Heh, heh.
So perhaps thou shalt feel good
about Root.
He cometh for thee.
He is the first to cometh for thee.
If thou canst manage it
just tarry awhile
and let Root and me
impregnate you with love,
for we must leave you
something to remember us by.

BAWDYHOUSE

No lethargy here. A place
that's just right
to put down for the night.
How much do they charge?
Girls are extra, I know.
What? No, I don't
use that kind of candy.
Keep it for yourself,
along with your razorblades
and little mirror.
I am a drunk,
not a dope fiend.
I am an acolyte of love,
and the instrument of flesh
that channels my love
might not be able to function
if I exposed him to too
many pollutants. So
keep your drugs, I'll
just have a Negro Modello
to cut the dust, and a
lady with the light in her eyes
to share some energy with.

THE KID

Let The Kid ride. By God,
let him ride. We need him,
and he *will* show up again.
It's a matter of accepting him
and shaking his hand,
or being shot down by him
when you reject him.

Wanted posters . . .
good for toilet paper, perhaps.
The Kid wipes his ass on
wanted posters, then leaves
them in the mailbox
at a church, or
taped to a squad car.
The straights don't actually
want The Kid,
the straights want to be
rid of The Kid.
But here he comes.
His death was only temporary.
In fact, he never dies at all.
He rides a wave of destruction,
and the illusions he rides over die,
but he doesn't. Hell, he's killed
his own damn illusions, you can't
expect him to give a damn about
yours.

Don't be shallow. When you reject
The Kid, you reject the most
vital part of yourself, the
part that's absolutely essential
for doing the work that has
to be done on
this earthplane.
Evil must be destroyed and
forever barred from
this planet.
You can't fight evil
without The Kid.

IMAGE BREAKER

Dance with me. What?
Oh. Yes, you're right.
That idol's in the way.
Here, have a glass of
juice, and I'll go
destroy the idol.
Then we can dance.

LOVE, THE IDEAL

Humour me. Imagine with me
a world in which
LOVE
is the ideal.
Please be aware of what I've just said:
I didn't say we should be more sentimental,
or controlling,
or emotionally irresponsible
or unbalanced.
I DID NOT say
we should be ruled
by our emotions (I didn't say we
should repress them, either.).

I am encouraging LOVE as the ideal.
Actual love, not the sloppy emotional
fluctuation the sentimental confuse with love.
That 's not love. That's just the lack of
discipline of the emotionally polarized.
Actual LOVE is a blessed force,
that comes straight from the Heart of God
to our hearts. Not to
our emotions, but to our hearts.
(Yes, if a person has enough emotional and mental
discipline, they can learn to reflect
their love thru their emotional and
mental bodies, but we aren't dealing
with that here. Go see your guru for
more information, then knock him in
the head with a stick of stove wood,
since you don't need a guru anyway,
and anyone who poses as a guru
is a phoney. If you meet the
Buddha on the road, set an anti-
personnel mine in his path.)

Mental fluctuations . . . perhaps I need
to exercise more discipline regarding my
digressions.

LOVE: If love were the ideal,
and if the people of the earth

exercised enough discipline
to keep their attention on this ideal,
then they would begin to draw
closer to this ideal. I don't
know how long it would take, but
since the nature of Humanity is LOVE,
maybe we would reach the point of
the manifestation of genuine Human Nature
pretty soon, if only we all held love before ourselves
as the supreme ideal.

Part of the problem is
that people believe they know
what love is. They don't.
No more than a handful
of human beings
has ever been able to reflect
the light of love into the world.
And many of that handful
were tortured or put to death
by the sentimental people,
those who feel they know love,
but who actually are in the grip
of undignified emotion. (Or mental
self-justification, in the case of many
of the controllers in positions
of authority. Self-
justification is childish and is
not the proper use
of the mental faculty. Moral
discrimination is proper, as
is the quest for the illumination
of spiritual truth.)

You know, in terms of a saint's ability
to preserve his physical incarnation,
there's nothing more dangerous
than an overly emotional human being
who feels he understands Love,
or some other Divine Principle such as
Justice. If he actually meets
a reflection of Love,
he may want to form a mob
to tar and feather the Divine Reflection
and ride him out of town on a rail.

(Or at least charge him with a felony. After
all, he *has* to do something to satisfy
that quaint squirming in his guts
that screams for ***Control!***)

Tell me something: do you believe
Jerry Falwell and the Pope of Rome
and others of their ilk
are reflections of LOVE?
Do you?
Or are they emotionally fluctuating
(sometimes emotionally frozen)
people who lack a true discipline?
Do they have the discipline to reflect
the discipline of the heart, which is LOVE?
Do they shine like Jesus? Then how
can they represent Him? And if they
don't represent Jesus, then what do they
represent? Pretty clothes and skullcaps and
huge institutions? Did Jesus
represent any institution?

A theology degree
is no substitute for love.

The Arabs and Israelis would
eventually solve their problems
if both sides accepted LOVE
as the ideal.
Presently, neither side has any
use for that ideal, despite
the fact that LOVE is
the only true ideal
for our earth humanity.

Sometimes people get
so frustrated and hurt
they can't begin
to imagine what love is,
and then all that's left to
them is vengeance.
But vengeance is never
a substitute for love.
Listen: nobody can deny
you love. Love is free,

and there's a place in your heart
where it resides, and when
you unlock that door
you will be born into the
Kingdom of Heaven.
And this is true
whether you're an Arab or an Israeli.

INITIATION

Behold, a door slams shut!
Which way to turn?
Rags to riches to rags.
Renunciation on the heels of abundance.
Equilibrium.

HYMN OF THE LONGHAIR

Turn loose of everything and ride, just ride.
Ride the winds of internal endurance
and fortitude. Make it holy
with sacrifice.
Be sacrifice.

Thou art no hippie. Thou shalt
not party down, dude.
To ride the inner breath,
the storm of all creation,
is enough of a high.
Too much of a high,
at times.

Lift the mountain.
Carry the mountain
from one end of the country
to the other. Find
your strength, you'll
need it. The longhair
Jesus couldn't have said
that faith moves mountains.
That's a passive, pansy thing
to say, and Jesus was no wimp.
He must've said that with
strength you
can move mountains, or
with intention you can
move mountains.
Faith is a pansy thing,
and Jesus was no pansy.
Jesus was--Jesus *is*--
strong.
Jesus moved his mountains with strength.
Jesus learned the power of a genuine, focused intention.

Go fishing in the Ganges,
bathe in it, too. Turn on
to Shiva, dig his scene
for a while, and pretty
soon, longhair, you'll
wish you were some old
grandpa sitting on a porch

with a crewcut and a pouch
of tobacco and a few wives.
Shiva is *harsh*, bubba. But
it's all for a good cause.
The destruction of Shiva
is beautiful, and uncovers
love. Shiva gets rid of
illusions so we can feel
and know the love which
we truly are. Then there's
that elephant of his . . .
you can either ride on his
back, or get run over by
him. He's a good ally.

ZENMAN

You any kin to me, Zenman?

touched with clear light

moving into the valley.

There's nothing there.

www.ingramcontent.com/pod-product-compliance
Lightning Source LLC
LaVergne TN
LVHW021347080426
835508LV00020B/2149